The Gift of Christ

Is Love

An anthology of Christian Poetry

edited by

Betty Madill

Blue Butterfly Publishers
Inverurie
Aberdeenshire AB51 4ZR
Scotland, UK

Published
November 2006

ISBN

0-9550642-2-8

978-0-9550642-2-7

The New Born Bairnie

Unheedin o the wins that sooch an blaw
His mither sittin prood like an sae brave
The new born bairnie's sleepin in a staa

She taks him tae her breist, content his craa
He nuzzles there, his steekit knievies wave
Unheedin o the wins that sooch an blaw

Some shepherds hear the news in fear an awe
Doon tae the byre they skelp wi crook an stave
The new born bairnie's sleepin in a staa

King Herod sens three wise men fine an brave
"Fin oot aboot that littlin" is his crave
Unheedin o the wins that sooch an blaw

Wi myrrh an gowd an frankincense they faa
Upon their knees in homage wi the lave
The new born bairnie's sleepin in a staa

His destiny obscure, an enigma
Oblivious tae the world he's come tae save
Unheedin o the wins that sooch an blaw
The new born bairnie's sleepin in a staa

Margaret Grant

See glossary

A mother-sauce

Cannelloni,
Settled in the slim white dish
Like funeral placements in a cramped hall
Await their final anointment,
The mother-sauce.

Walnuts,
Tree knuckles knocking together
Like a clatter of wizard worry-beads
Ground into a bitty paste,
The Liturgy.

Tomatoes,
Ripe plum plump dumplings
Like Ferrari festoons spilt from a jar,
Tumbling through the chancel
Choir from afar.

Under Ferrara cathedral's crossed roofing struts:
Basil, olives, oregano and cloves
Resurrected from Italian groves,
Buttered creamed pampered and wined
Pasta and sauce
Feed scripture and mind.

                                        Phil Fox

Eden: Jack Clemo's Clay-Pit

Why do we stand where feet have stood before,
to puddle clay and work this barren soil?
Snow-coloured mountains urge us to explore

what can be done with rusting waste and spoil.
The Cornish stars have witnessed blood from stone:
red wood bears scars of sacrificial toil.

How can we claim a kingdom for our own?
This aching realm, which thorns have prised apart,
shows seeds of hope as tangled weeds bow down.

Where is this place where nature turns to art?
Our pit of tears is shaped by history:
its mine still yields rich treasures of the heart

when we receive God's grace, confront those scars
and reap in joy fresh signs of victory.
We find new life in Eden's land of stars,
where clay was fashioned for eternity.

                                                            Caroline Gill

Pray

She was smooth black svelte
Shone mauve from head to toe
As I looked from the gleaming polished shoes
To the black suit, the dark-hued chiffon scarf
And her face, red-lipped, smiling in repose
The eyes mocked, half-hidden, behind the shades
And her hair glistened, swung at her shoulders
As long fingers, thick silver bands shining
Moved slowly against the white page
Of the book held loosely there

It was bright, crisp, new bought
Gleamed its title as the page turned
Urging its importance, a shrill command
In massive type *Think and Grow Rich*
And what I couldn't understand, what snagged
What drew me back to stare and stare again?
Forgetting the passing stations, stuck fast
In the mystery drama of this other life, was
The leather bookmark flat on the white page
Which said simply *Pray*

Charles Evans

Yesterday, Today and Tomorrow

Night opens cosmos-sized gates,
lets slip a tiny spool of light,
and Christ is born of Mary –
whilst the Earth is at its farthest
oscillating feint pulsed-point.

Through fire and ice
avoiding meteors, comets
and black-holes,
the child ignites souls to life.

So cold to-day
as though for a second
God changed his mind
withheld Christ's birth;

a nuclear winter prevents the Gloria.
The precious star of Bethlehem
lost in the mists of the Milky Way –
drifts past Earth.

And we are waiting in open fields,
faces upturned, searching clouds,
whilst all the while He lies in a manger;
the sweet child of the universe,
opening His eyes to inferior copies
of his heavenly hosts.

Pauline Hawkesworth

Dressing The Tree

Finding pine needles in the carpet
in mid-summer
reminds me of dressing the tree.

Each year I haul home
a small fir from the forest
in the market;
my gloved hands smarting.

Each year we buy a new ornament:
A delicate glass bell,
a thick twist of tinsel,
a tiny angel with a golden trumpet...

Each year I get down the magic box
from the attic,
work out the wink and flash of fairy lights,
while you unwrap silver and red and blue,

...and each year, I point out
the old decorations which belong to me
and we laugh as we loop and thread
and hang my childhood on the tree.

When you are grown I shall give you:
the delicate glass bell,
the thick twist of tinsel,
the tiny angel with the golden trumpet...

hand you down the legacy of joy
in finding pine needles...
and, in dressing the tree.

Denise Bennett

Things to do for Christmas

Let Gabriel tell Virgin Mary she is carrying
child called Jesus - Son of God -
say Joseph, her spouse, won't mind.
Get Caesar to call people to Bethlehem.
Order donkey. Polish star.
Tell innkeeper to prepare stable for birth.
Line manger with hay for baby.
Dazzle shepherds, lead them to Jesus.
Guide three wise men to Herod –
enrage him because they haven't come
to worship him.
Arrange gifts - gold - frankincense – myrrh.
Let wise men kneel before Saviour.
Warn Joseph in dream Herod
intends killing male babies.
Let Mary, Joseph, Jesus escape.

Denise Bennett

Blind Faith

Corseted in self-righteous Christianity,
clad in the armour of God
with breast-plate chaste and polished,
she stood sentinel at the entrance to the church,
the welcoming committee of one.
Prising open her frosted lips,
while glacial eyes assessed me, sinner,
the icicles spelt out "Good Morning."
Clean and manicured
her hand held out a leaflet,
"Welcome to our Church."
She let me pass
and closed the door
upon the outside world.

Her halo scrubbed with virtue
she settled in her cushioned pew
and raised her head
to hear the minister intone familiar words.
"Though I speak with the tongues of men
and of angels,
and have not charity,
I am become as sounding brass,
or a tinkling cymbal."

Marjorie A Mitchell

You think it odd

You think it odd,
we share some bread.
We talk of God.

I see you nod,
something I said?
You think it odd?

The way less trod
we choose instead.
We talk of God.

I feel unshod
and filled with dread;
you think it odd.

It's hard, we plod,
'For us He bled';
we talk of God.

Leave it unsaid
before we're dead?
You think it odd;
we talk of God.

                    Richard Broadhurst

Prayers

Sometimes a child, preoccupied, at play,
looks up inquiringly, eyes full of zest,
absorbed and vital, brimming with the best
that you'll experience that day.
Sometimes in Tweedsmuir, turning a bend,
a mighty oak confronts you, magnificently,
its branches oblations as cloudscapes in the sky
accumulate, hymning a world without end.
Sometimes poetry from the blank page leaps,
and clusters of minims and semibreves speak
of the ultimate light and sweetness that you seek,
the central harmony where the infinite sleeps.
Each can illuminate, each play a part.
Aspects of prayer: life, nature, poetry, art.

Norman Bissett

Paradox

Who needs zombies or vampires?

At quantum-level nothing is alive,
we are walking piles of dust;
we are all *the living dead.*

It's hard for witches
and warlocks, physicists muscling in
on the old, mythological words,
standing magic on its head.
I like toting around
my own inanimate atoms.

I love the oddness:

heaving along the ancient data,
elements and stars
packed into an arm and a leg;
the irony
that hard-nosed scientists
accept this paradox,
(such a metaphysical phrase,)

yet scorn any concepts of God.

Isobel Thrilling

Best of the rest…

Prayer

Our father
Who possibly at this moment in time
Could be in heaven figuratively speaking,
All credit to you. Let your performance targets
Be met in accordance with the policy objective.
Get a result, ensuring benefits for everyone at
Grass roots, and us too when we reach our
Sell-by date. Give us all we want 24/7 and
Make allowances when we over-react as
We do for our opponents. And don't
Give us any aggravation but keep
Us all from under-performing.
It's a great system
With authority
And prestige
Indefinitely
Cheers

                                Charles Evans

Tell It Again

It is told and retold, the story
of Mary and her child;
and our smallest ones still listen
eyes widening as they hear
of angels, shepherds, kings;
strange tales for urban ears,
like genies in the pantomime,
flying carpets, cats that talk
and little monster men from Mars.

At school they recreate the play
with tinsel haloes, plastic lambs
carols and stars; anxious and excited
to please proud parents, favourite teachers,
and inherit Santa's bounty.

Some understand with knowledge
what the times were like –
the refugee that no-one wants
whose mother struggles
with a newborn sibling
in a makeshift hut in a flooded camp:
a child for whom no angels sing,
no shepherds watch, no kings bring gold.

The star of hope is clouded
by the smoke of burning homes,
and cries of orphans drown the music
of the heavenly host.
The message that the angels brought
is buried in complacency,
left unattended in the shopping mall,
caught in the snares of cybernetic games.

We drop our conscience money
in a Sally Army tin, but close our doors
to sad reminders of those people left outside.
Will we do any better this year,
next year, any year?
or just repeat the old, old story?

                                        Edna Eglinton

Shroud of Silence

One day each year, in autumn,
after Fireworks and before The Carols,
everyone wore poppies and we stood
in silent rows behind our desks.

Traffic stopped.
Shops, trains, factories were still.
Time froze. Mothers went inside
and closed their doors.

Silence filled our classroom
like a weight of attic-dust and camphor.
Teacher clenched her eyes
and on her cheeks we saw slow tears.

After the cannon's boom released us
she explained - by this act of silence
we would keep the world from falling
back into war and pain.

But before my schooldays were completed
we had failed her. The magic was annulled.
The rite proved worthless.
Silence was not enough.

They chiselled names in stone again
and spoke of glory. They dazzled us
with lures of happy-ever-after,
soothed us with valium.

Two generations later, myths and demons
rise through cyber-space, become reality.
Young minds, imprisoned by our silence
are unprepared to find real killing hurts.

Edna Eglinton

Who's Crazy?

Crazy - we'd say if she told us
an angel spoke.
She pondered it in her heart,
knew it was true.

Crazy - your great grandfather
would say
if he saw you with your mobile
talking, listening.

Crazy - if we could tell him
how we watch pictures
in our sitting rooms
coming from around the world,

and that all the knowledge
ever written
comes instantly to view
at the touch of a plastic mouse!

We believe what The Papers tell us;
We are duped by a fast-talk salesman;
We know what we think is possible;
So Angels ? - that's fantasy!

Edna Eglinton

Of His Own We Give

Thunder was silent;
Earth was dark;
Chaos moved.

Though stars were spinning
all their light escaped.

Transparency of seraphim
surrounding crystal thrones
let the glory slip between them
and away.

Until he made the human race,
until our finite shapes began
to block his light
our bold Creator's plan
remained unseen.

Our diverse angles turn from him
refracting light to colour;
our density substantiates
his bright unclouded form;

our senses set a limit to vibrations
that we hear as music;
we index all dimensions
as only space and time;

we confine his dancing atoms
to agree with our perceptions
then block his helping hand
with pride.

We twist his laws to suit our purpose;
spread his light in broken patterns;
in return we give him bold distortions
of his own reflection.

Edna Eglinton

Though It Tarries, It Will Come

Person:	Oh God forgive me for my selfish nature I'm struggling Lord! I'm such a mess!
Person:	Oh God, have you forsaken me?
God:	No my child, just be patient
Person:	But Lord I feel like the last train has gone And I'm still waiting at the station
God:	Follow my decrees, follow my ways Trust in Me! I am the Ancient of Days
Person:	Oh God, have you forsaken me?
God:	No my child. You are unique
Person:	But I don't seem to be going forward Have I already reached my peak?
God:	There are mountains you have yet to climb Trust in Me! I am divine.
Person:	Oh God, you have forsaken me! I can't hear your voice
God:	My child I am speaking to your heart But it's up to you to make a choice
God:	Choose now this day whom you will serve

Person: Oh Lord, can I just have a sign?

God: I sent my Son to die on a cross
             (Read John 19 verse 1 to 39)

God: My child, My yoke is easy, My burden light
             Come to Me and I will give you rest

God: For I am the Lord! I am divine!
             Trains will always leave the station
             But wait for Me. I am always on time.
                            Cherron Inko-Tariah

Magi

Thirty years ago, I sat in this house,
hearing, as now, night wind in the chimney,
knowing the magi had gone, gone away.
Useless for a demented king to chase
them that weather, so many paths to choose
on the downs, sea too loud for company
on the coast. And one thought among many
they shared with changing sky and kept its peace.

I think the magi do not hear the wind,
beating ground like a carpet now, much less
the screams that are wrapped in it, in the wires'
wailing. They have gone back to their own land
having found a way through that map of stars
while parents of dead children tend their loss.

Ian Caws

The shepherds

What did the shepherds think, chatting at nine,
When they heard angels in song?
"They'd had too much of the cheering mulled wine,
Helping the cold night along!"

What did they think when they saw the Three Kings
Riding in splendour their way?
They must have thought they're imagining things -
Actors dressed up in a play.

What did they think in the stable that night -
Miracles just didn't end!
Angels and kings in celestial light -
Mary had Jesus to tend.

And what did they think such a long time ago
On that first cold Christmas Day
As they trudged back to their flocks in the snow?
How could they think what to say?

Can we explain just what happened that day,
Clever and wise as we are?
Let us sing carols and gratefully pray,
Trust and just follow the Star!

Anthony C. Payne

Unwrapping Christmas

Christmas comes in magic wrapped.
What magic?
Nostalgia, in snowy scenes,
Victorian warmth around the log fire hearth,
Home transformed to dreamland
With lights and colours,
Children's excitement and expectancy
At ribbons, wrappings, parcels round the tree
Giving and goodwill in hearts of men,
Smiles, despite the hardness,
Pain and disillusion of the years,
God's name on every lip in song,
Angels, wise men, shepherds
A part of daily life - this century when God is dead?
What is the magic of a mystery?
Unwrap the magic
See the mystery
Transcending history
Eternity reaching into time
The mightiest event of heaven performed
On earth with shame and scorn.
Joy to the world which cannot see.
Unwrap the magic
And fall in awe before Him
In worship
Inexpressible rejoicing
Of a human heart tasting love divine.

Sheila Longman

How Truly Lucky I Am

"Let us pray" the minister said
I closed my eyes and bowed my head
We prayed for those in countries at war
Suffering, innocent children wondering `what for'
The poor, the starving in drought ridden land
Land which was fertile and is now only sand
We prayed for all those who are ill
Who won't get any better, never will
For criminals who have committed a crime
Now in a prison, serving time
For the victims, the families, those left bereft
For just about everyone, hardly anyone left

I thought of myself, happy and healthy
Just an ordinary person, not very wealthy
As we sang the 23rd Psalm
I thought, how truly lucky I am.

Anne Logan

Northern Christmas

The winter sky held a million stars.
The air was clear and cold,
A sea breeze crooned among the waves
Its lullaby of old.

Some fishers in their fragile boat,
Rocked by the ocean tide,
Gazed up in awe as a falling star
Flashed silver as it died.

And far away across the firth,
Where the mountains greet the sea,
Wives and bairns exhausted sleep,
In their hovels by the quay.

How could they know in a distant land
The Christ Child had been born?
For them a rest from grinding toil,
Before another dawn.

No angels sang them of His birth,
No shepherds with their sheep,
No Magi with their gifts of gold,
No Holy Infant fast asleep.

For them the darkness still held sway,
Till centuries went by,
Before the blessed light of Truth
Lit up their northern sky.

No need of stars to light the path,
To guide them on their way,
To where the holy angels sing
Before Him night and day.

                              Edward Mitchell

What 'Peace' is this?

What `peace' is this
that sand-papers a person
right down to their original grain;
removes multi-layers
of varnish and paint?

This `peace'
lands as a shuttle from space,
bringing its cargo of apostles
to examine, heal, eat and drink;
announcing precious swaddling news –
the Kingdom of God is near.

The powerful peace
presses home God's message;
and we play the new self again
and again, love its strong touch
and how light glitters
on each slightly raised nodule
that makes us all different.

Pauline Hawkesworth

Oronsay Prior
(for Susanna)

I came as a pilgrim
with little time to spare
a few mere minutes
before the tide turned there

Some say it was here
St. Columba first came
to preach, to heal
in the words of love
the life of Christ the man

Tranquility and peace
is your soul
through centuries of prayer
a place so silent,
so spiritually aware

I pass through to the chapel
and there, the altar bare
I lay my hand on the cold stone
to be with you
silently,
          in my prayer
                         Julie Rutherford

Services

Humbly he takes our paper mugs away –
Then wipes the tables carefully…
An "Admiral Crichton verily.
Although I do not know his name,
To him I want say:-
"Thank you for shaking hands
in Church today
I too must clear up one Sunday
After Communion - when again
We join hands and say
'Peace be with you'.

Valerie Faith Irvine-Fortescue

After The Service, Coffee Will Be Served

The preacher's words have scarcely died away.
The organ's peal still echoes on the air.
The coffee's hardly poured or sugar stirred,
as eagerly the whispering begins.
"Oh, have you heard...
                    ...who she moved in with yesterday?
A shock for all her friends: at *her* age too.
Her husband too ashamed to show his face.
What's the world *coming* to?
And have you heard...?"
                    ...Oh yes,
and something else I've heard,
as we stand gossiping before the cross:
that Jesus Christ forgives all sins,
hers, yours and everyone's; and bids us not condemn.

"But have *you heard?* He lost his job, they say.
You never see *her* any more in church
(she drinks, you know). He's got a roving eye.
Resigned *his* job, they say: the push, more like.
Their daughter's into drugs; her son's no good.
And have you heard...?"
                    ...Oh yes,
and something else I've heard and pray it's true,
is that we Christians strive to be
more Christ-like in our thoughts, our words and deeds.
Because He died to save us all:
him, her, you, me and everyone...

Outside, the unrelenting rain might be Christ's tears...
                                        Michael Limmer

34

Emmanuel

Advent; time to reflect on Grace,
but preparations gather pace
and lives are bound with busyness;
while others struggle under stress.
When Christmas dawns, we rush to greet
Jesus, to make the day complete.
But is He left in manger cold?
And is the story yet untold
that God should come and with us dwell,
each one, our God, Emmanuel?
And every day and moment share
His presence in each trial and care.
Yet, do we shut Him out so soon
or fail to make, for Him, the room?

Hilary Allen

The Sleeping Butterfly

The Sleeping Butterfly
spreads his wings
and makes an arc:
It is called
...dreaming.

And the coloured pattern
of his wings
makes a kaleidoscope
in the eyes:
...dreaming.

And the kaleidoscope pattern
fills the eyes,
fill the mind's eye,
 ...dreaming.

The Sleeping Butterfly
flies across
the curtain
of the sleeping child,
and lifts the veil
to show its colour
 ...it is called dreaming.

                              Tricia Nolan

Christmas Present

Jolly old St Nicholas
was struggling to find
reasons to be joyful.
He's so much on his mind.

With war, with famine,
pain and death
and politicians' lies,
it's getting harder every year
to don the old disguise.

The velvet suit is packed away.
The long white beard clean shaved.
He looks out at this world and asks,
'Can Christmas still be saved?'

He wanders through the city streets
alive with tawdry lights.
They offer neither joy nor warmth
to brighten winter's nights.

He comes upon a stable yard,
aglow with candle flame.
He hears a mother whispering
her tiny baby's name.

With ox, with donkey,
sheep and lamb,
he contemplates the scene.
The spirit that is hope and love
sleeps soundly, all serene.

Jolly old St Nicholas,
his rosy face now beams.
That tiny child reminded him
what Christmas really means.

The suit, the beard,
the present sack
The open hearted giving
A gift for every Christmas child,
the gentle Grace of Heaven.

Catherine Lang

Hymn

Be you my Parent, dear Lord; understand
I need all your wisdom to hold on my hand.
When I am tearful, half-crazy, and weak,
Oh, grant me the saneness I think not to seek.

Be you my Playmate, who shares all my joy
In playing with friends with some frivolous toy,
In throwing a stick for a dog as it runs,
And springtime, and jokes, and ridiculous puns.

Be you the Artist all artists admire,
Who lights up our poems, as candles from fire.
Though you hide in shadows as source of our work,
The glow of your universe lights up the murk.

Pagans divide you: the female from male,
The god of the forge from the god of the flail,
The wisdom-god, sea-god – they chop you apart
To bits that will fit in my mind and my heart.

Great God of Heaven, oh, help me to see
There's room in your heart and your mind to love me,
For you are creator of both great and small –
Electrons and galaxies – master of all!

Elizabeth Bullen

Snow

Driving to the hospital
ignoring the warnings
not to venture out
on these roads,
knowing this man's prayers –
knowing this man –
would keep us safe
in his silence
in this snow.

Eve Jackson

Christmas Acrostic

C is for the Christ Child, who in the manger lay.
H   is for the hope He brings to children of The Way.
R is for His righteousness, which shows us how to be.
I   is for His innocence, which saves and sets us free.
S is for the songs we sing, in praise of His great worth.
T is for the Truth he brings to everyone on earth.
M is for Mary, His mother: dear to God's own heart.
A is for the angelic host, who also played their part.
S is for the songs they sang, announcing Royal Birth.

"Emmanuel - God with us, and Peace to men on Earth!"
Margaret Tutt

In Praise of Devotion

I   would live
in   the shade
of   the sign
that was made
when our Lord
gave his life
to   renounce
human   strife;
but I   praise and admire those who bravely aspire
to be moved by the splendour and light of his fire
to   great acts of devotion endurance and love
whose   courage and selflessness constantly   prove
there's a way
that redeems
us from fear
and   despair,
living proof
of the good
that endures
everywhere.
Their   lustre
and   courage
give strength
to   the rest;
the weakest
amongst   us
take   heart
from the best

Rex Andrews

42

Candles

Is there something plaintive about lighting candles?
Something that remains
When soot-smudges stain the white wax,
Weave into the smoke wisps,
Drawn upward
High through the chancel.
Touching someone's lit prayer.

Do chandlers mould mysteries into their candles?
Trawling thick wicks
Through a trough of hot slicking wax,
Rolling congealed fables,
Smoothed tubes
Sealing sagas in sage,
Burnishing the myth of care.

Phil Fox

Designer Shoes

I need
Designer shoes
Designer clothes
Designer life

I need
A new look
A new mobile
A new car

I need
A holiday abroad
A well paid job
A comfortable house

I need
Status
Recognition
Attention
Fulfilled ambition
A fairytale romance

Elizabeth needed a bag of maize
To feed her children with

                    Joan Shaw

Gye Near
(Almost here)

Come on, kep goin ma dearie,
we're gye near Bethlehem;
see oot ower, lowin lichts
an yatterin fowk roon fires;
kin ye hear e snickerin camels,
smell e stink o e yowes
an e soughin wind throu than palm trees
cweelin yer swytin chowks?

Sic a mineer shoot e place,
e chynge-hoose 'll be stowed oot:
mibbe e place for yer lyin-in
e byre amang e nowt?
fen sat first shour shoots throu
ye as e angels will sing in e lift
for jilt like it wis tellt ye,
this bairn is God's sin Gift.

Mary Johnston

See glossary

Glossary

The New Born Bairnie

bairnie	baby
wins	winds
blaw	blow
sooch	sigh, whistle
blaw	blow
prood	proud
briest	breast
staa	stall
briest	breast
craa	hunger, need
steekit	clenched
kneives	fists
skelp	dash, run
wi	with
sens	sends
gowd	gold
faa	fall
lave	the rest, the others

Gye Near

gye near	almost there
oot ower	in the distance
lowin	glowing
yatterin	chattering
yowes	ewe sheep
soughin	sighing
cweelin	cooling
swytin	sweating
chowks	cheeks
sic	such
miner	confusion
chynge-hoose	inn
stowed oot	crowded out
lyin-in	confinement
nowt	cattle
fen	when
shour	labour pain
lift	sky
o' e	of the
roon	round